Affirmations for the Soul

Praise be to God,
who fills our hearts
with joy and our lips
with song.

Let our praises rise like incense before the throne of the Almighty.

In the presence of the Lord, let gratitude overflow from every corner of our souls.

May our worship be a sweet melody that resonates in the heavens.

With hearts lifted high, we exalt the name of our Savior.

In awe and wonder, we stand before the majesty of our Creator.

Every breath we take
is a testament to the
goodness of our God.

With hands uplifted, we surrender to the love that knows no bounds.

In the quiet moments of worship, let His peace reign supreme.

Let the rhythm of our praise be a reflection of His grace.

As we sing, let every note be a declaration of His faithfulness.

In the beauty of holiness, we find our truest expression of worship.

With humble hearts, we offer our praises as a fragrant offering.

In His presence, chains are broken, and hearts are set free.

Let our worship be
an offering of
thanksgiving for all
He has done.

In the sanctuary of praise, we find renewal and strength.

With voices united, we proclaim the greatness of our God.

In the midst of storms, our worship becomes an anchor for the soul.

With reverence and awe, we bow before the King of Kings.

May our worship echo throughout eternity, bringing glory to His name.

In every season, we will sing of His unwavering love.

Our hearts are lifted as we gaze upon the beauty of the Lord.

Let the light of His glory shine through our worship.

In the stillness, we hear the whispers of His grace.

Our worship is a response to the wonder of His works.

With hearts ablaze,
we celebrate the
goodness of our God.

In His presence, we
find fullness of joy
and peace.

Every song we sing is

an anthem of His

great love.

Let our worship be a beacon of hope to the world.

In the shadow of His wings, we find our refuge.

Our praise rises like
a mighty river,
flowing to the throne
of grace.

In the light of His presence, darkness has no place.

With every breath, we declare His greatness and mercy.

In worship, we encounter the heart of the Father.

Our songs of praise
are a testimony to
His faithfulness.

Let our worship be a declaration of His eternal truth.

In the company of angels, we join the chorus of heaven.

With hearts wide open, we embrace the love of our Savior.

Our worship is a celebration of His victory over the grave.

In the depths of worship, we find our true identity in Him.

Every act of worship is a step closer to His heart.

In His presence, we are transformed and renewed.

With a spirit of gratitude, we offer our praises to the King.

Let our worship be a reflection of His boundless grace.

In the sanctuary of His presence, we are made whole.

Our praise is a weapon against the forces of darkness.

With joy in our hearts, we sing of His endless love.

In worship, we
encounter the power
and majesty of our
God.

Let our voices be lifted high, proclaiming His holiness.

In every moment of praise, we draw nearer to His heart.

Our hearts are vessels, filled with the overflow of His love.

In His presence, every worry fades away.

With every chord, we celebrate the splendor of our King.

In worship, we find strength for the journey ahead.

Our praise is a
fragrant offering,
rising to His throne.

In the embrace of His love, we are forever changed.

Let our worship be a testament to His everlasting mercy.

In the sanctuary of praise, we find peace for our souls.

Our songs are declarations of His unmatched greatness.

With hearts united,
we lift a symphony of
praise.

In His presence, we find healing and restoration.

Our worship is a tapestry woven with threads of gratitude.

In the light of His glory, all shadows flee.

Let every word of praise be a tribute to His goodness.

In the beauty of His holiness, we stand in awe.

Our worship is a journey into the heart of God.

With each note, we proclaim His majestic power.

In His presence, our souls find their true home.

Our praise is a declaration of His unchanging love.

With every breath,

we honor the

King of Kings.

In the midst of our worship, His presence is made known.

Our hearts sing of His mercy and grace.

In worship, we
encounter the depths
of His love.

With joyful hearts,
we lift our voices in
praise.

In the stillness, we hear His gentle whisper.

Our worship is an offering of our deepest devotion.

In His presence, we are enveloped in His peace.

Let our songs be a reflection of His unfailing love.

In worship, we find our true purpose and calling.

Our praise is a response to the wonders of His creation.

In the light of His presence, our hearts are renewed.

With each act of worship, we draw closer to His heart.

In the sanctuary of praise, we find our strength.

Our worship is a celebration of His boundless love.

In His presence, we are made whole and complete.

With hearts full of gratitude, we lift our songs to Him.

In worship, we experience the fullness of His joy.

Our praise is a reflection of His eternal faithfulness.

In the quiet moments, we are touched by His grace.

Our worship is a testament to His unwavering love.

In His presence, we find our true identity.

With every song, we declare His endless mercy.

In the beauty of worship, we are transformed.

Our praise is an offering of our deepest love.

In the light of His glory, we find our peace.

With hearts surrendered, we lift our voices in praise.

In worship, we encounter the depth of His compassion.

Our songs are echoes
of His everlasting
love.

In the stillness of His presence, we find rest.

Our worship is a celebration of His infinite grace.

Oh Bless my Soul with Praise and Worship.

Fill my soul with Praise and Thanksgiving.

May your Soul be

blessed with each

message of Love !

Jeannette Golden